First World War
and Army of Occupation
War Diary
France, Belgium and Germany

59 DIVISION
178 Infantry Brigade
Sherwood Foresters
(Nottinghamshire and Derbyshire Regiment)
2/6th Battalion
2 November 1914 - 26 February 1916

WO95/3025/2

The Naval & Military Press Ltd
www.nmarchive.com
Published in association with The National Archives

Published by

The Naval & Military Press Ltd

Unit 10 Ridgewood Industrial Park,

Uckfield, East Sussex,

TN22 5QE England

Tel: +44 (0) 1825 749494

www.naval-military-press.com

www.nmarchive.com

This diary has been reprinted in facsimile from the original. Any imperfections are inevitably reproduced and the quality may fall short of modern type and cartographic standards.

© **Crown Copyright**
Images reproduced by permission of The National Archives, London, England, 2015.

Contents

Document type	Place/Title	Date From	Date To
Heading	WO 3025 59th Div 2/6 BN Sherwood Foresters 1914 Nov-1916 Feb		
Heading	59 Div 178 Bde 2/6 Bn Sherwood Foresters 1914 Nov-1916 Feb		
Heading	War Diaries Of 2/6th Sherwood Foresters November To December 1914		
War Diary	Buxton.	02/11/1914	30/11/1914
Miscellaneous	2/6th Bn. The Sherwood Foresters.		
War Diary	Buxton.	29/12/1914	30/12/1914
Miscellaneous	2/6th Bn. The Sherwood Foresters.		
Heading	War Diaries Of 2/6th Sherwood Foresters January To April and September To December 1915		
Miscellaneous	British Salonika Force War Diary		
War Diary	Buxton.	01/01/1915	31/01/1915
Miscellaneous	2/6th Bn. The Sherwood Foresters.		
War Diary	Buxton.	03/02/1915	03/02/1915
War Diary	Luton.	07/02/1915	08/02/1915
War Diary	Epping.	09/02/1915	24/02/1915
War Diary	Luton.	25/02/1915	25/02/1915
Miscellaneous	2/6th Bn. The Sherwood Foresters.		
War Diary	Luton.	02/03/1915	20/03/1915
Miscellaneous	2/6th Bn, The Sherwood Foresters.		
War Diary	Luton.	08/04/1915	27/04/1915
Miscellaneous	2/6th. Bn. The Sherwood Foresters.		
War Diary	Watford.	01/09/1915	30/09/1915
Miscellaneous	2/6th Bn. The Sherwood Foresters.		
War Diary	Watford.	01/10/1915	31/10/1915
Miscellaneous	2/6th Battn. The Sherwood Foresters.		
War Diary	Watford.	02/11/1915	30/11/1915
Miscellaneous	2/6th Bn. The Sherwood Foresters.		
War Diary	Watford.	01/12/1915	29/12/1915
Miscellaneous	2/6th. Bn. The Sherwood Foresters.	07/01/1915	07/01/1915
Heading	War Diary Of 2/6th Bn. Sherwood Foresters From 1st To 31st January 1916. Volume		
War Diary	Watford	06/01/1916	31/01/1916
Heading	War Diary Of 2/6th Bn, The Sherwood Foresters.		
Heading	War Diary Of 2/6th Bn. The Sherwood Foresters From 1st To 29th February 1916. Volume. XVI		
War Diary	Watford.	02/02/1916	26/02/1916
Miscellaneous	2/6th. Bn. The Sherwood Foresters.		

WO 3025
59th DIV

2/6 BN SHERWOOD
FORESTERS

1914 Nov - 1916 Feb

59 DIV

178 BDE

2/6 BN SHERWOOD FORESTERS

1914 NOV — 1916 FEB
1916 FEB

War diaries of
2/6th Sherwood Foresters.

November & December
1914.

Army Form C. 2118.

WAR DIARY
or
INTELLIGENCE SUMMARY.
(Erase heading not required.)

2/6th Bn. The Sherwood Foresters.

Place	Date	Hour	Summary of Events and Information	Remarks and references to Appendices
BUXTON.	1914. Novr. 2nd		Established Headquarters, Empire Hotel, Buxton. Arrivals, 182 men.	
"	5th		1 N.C.O. and 15 men reported their arrival from 6th Bn. Sherwood Foresters, Harpenden.	
"	10th		Clr.Sgt.Instr. Keery reported his arrival from the 6th Bn. Sherwood Foresters, Happenden and became Regimental Sergeant Major. 1 N.C.O. and 119 men departed for the 1st Reinforcement to 6th Bn., Harpenden.	
"	11th		1 N.C.O. and 9 men from the 6th Bn., Harpenden, reported their arrival.	
"	19th		The Battalion attended a Memorial Service to the late Field Marshal Earl Roberts at the Parish Church, Buxton.	
"	26th		12 men departed to 6th Bn., Braintree.	
"	30th		200 M.L.E. Rifles received.	

2/6th Bn. The Sherwood Foresters.

2/6TH BN. THE SHERWOOD FORESTERS.

STATEMENT.
NOVEMBER 1914.

FORMATION OF THE BATTALION.

The 2/6th Bn. Sherwood Foresters was recruited during the month of October 1914 at the Headquarters, Drill Hall, Chesterfield, and the various Company Headquarters throughout the 6th Battn. area.

On October 14th, 1914, Lieut. Col. J.M.Clayton, T.D., relinquished the command of the 6th Bn. Sherwood Foresters and returned to Chesterfield to raise and command the Reserve Unit.

He brought with him Capt.Welch who temporarily took charge of the Depot at Chesterfield, and was promoted Major on October 14th, 1914, Capt V.H.E.Langford was appointed Adjutant. Quartermaster Sergt. W.J.Roberts appointed Quartermaster and Hon.Lieut.

The men, as they were enrolled, were sent back to their homes and were paid 3/- per day, inclusive billet allowance and pay, plus 3d. per day for clothing, until they were equipped and clothed.

Some attempt was made to teach the men elementary squad drill, but owing to the shortage of Officers and N.C.O's., and the fact that all the experienced men were busily employed recruiting, little could be done in this direction until the men were called up.

On November 2nd, 1914, the Headquarters of the Battalion were established at Buxton. 184 men were clothed at the Depot, Chesterfield, on that day and despatched to Buxton. The remainder were called up, clothed and despatched to Buxton in Drafts daily.

CLOTHING.

The clothing was supplied by the County Territorial Association, and the men were clothed as they were called up.

Clr. Sergt. Inst. Keery from the 6th Battn. arrived at Buxton on November 10th, 1914, and the work of organising and training the recruits was proceeded with.

The establishment of the Battalion was 977 N.C.O's. and men, and this was completed by the end of November. 26 N.C.O's. and men reported from the 6th Battn. during the month.

From November to February 1915, 50 men were found permanently unfit for service and were discharged.

It cannot be said that the medically unfit from the 1st Line materially affected the training of the remainder. In many instances very useful work was done by medically unfit N.C.O's. in training recruits.

RECRUITING.

This was carried out by canvas and meetings. There was a distinct preference shown by recruits for a Territorial Battn. where they would be serving with their own friends, and the satisfactory nature of recruiting is shown from the fact that the Battn. was raised to full strength in a month.

When the 3rd Line was formed in February and March there was considerable clashing with the recruiting for the Regular Army. The recruiting Staff of the Regular Army did not look with favour on the Territorials recruiting in the areas over which they had control, and some little friction occurred. When the first rush of recruits to join had spent itself the difficulties of recruiting in competition with the organisation of the Regular Army Staffs were much increased.

(2)

RECRUITING (contd).

The factor which enabled the Territorials to obtain the men required, was the preference of the recruits to serve in a local Battalion amongst men drawn from their own towns and districts.

A Band would have helped recruiting at the start, and every effort was made to obtain one by Lieut.Col. J.M.Clayton. He succeeded on November 20th, 1914, in enlisting the New Mills Prize Band en block, and the Band brought their own instruments. The excellent music played by the Band at Buxton at the head of the Battalion not only quickly influenced the marching of the men, but stimulated recruiting at Buxton in other branches of His Majesty's Army.

A Few men were cast in the early days for being under height, but later most of these men enlisted in Bantam Battalions.

Considering the number of men enlisting the work of the civilian medical men was done excellently, and every care was taken to ensure the acceptance of only the physically fit.

The issue on attestation of full kit and equipment would not have induced further men to join.
The Battalion was clothed expeditiously. At the same time experience has shown that men after being enrolled do not like to be sent home to return to their work while waiting the clothing and kit. They prefer to be called up immediately on enlistment.

SANITATION.

There was no difficulty in billets in regard to sanitation, as the men were billeted in their own homes.

At the Empire Hotel, Buxton, under the supervision of Capt. Duncan, R.A.M.C., the Medical Officer, urinals and latrines were erected in the gardens in covered wood and corrugated iron sheds. Water carriage with intermittent automatic flush was installed and Inspecting Officers frequently expressed their

SANITATION (contd).

approval of these excellent sanitary arrangements.
The appointment of a D.O.R.E. would not have assisted.
Every help was rendered by the Buxton M.O.H. and Sanitary Inspector.

DRAFTS.

45 men were sent on November 5th, 1914, to the 1st Line Unit from Chesterfield, 120 men on November 9th from Buxton, and 12 men on November 26th from Buxton.

MESSING.

Messing took place in the large Garage in the grounds of the Hotel. Many difficulties had to be overcome at first in catering for the Battalion owing to a lack of utensils, but these were procured with despatch and the messing arrangements subsequently proved entirely satisfactory. There was a concrete floor to the garage, with a plentiful water supply from standpipes, and the whole place was daily swilled and scrubbed.

HOSPITAL ACCOMMODATION.

Several cases were sent to the 3rd Northern General Hospital, Sheffield, and Devonshire Hospital, Buxton. The local V.A.D. was entirely occupied by Belgian wounded. Slight cases were treated in Detention Room adjoining the Medical Inspection Room, a lofty, airy bedroom on first floor of Hotel. Hospital and Sanitary arrangements were inspected by the A.D.M.S. and Divisional Sanitary Officer on a surprise visit and satisfaction was expressed except as to certain billets in the basements of the Hotel, which was at once altered.

RIFLES.

200 M.L.E. Rifles were received on November 30th, and men suitable for promotion to N.C.O's. were immediately selected and put through a course of training in rifle exercises to facilitate the subsequent training of recruits.

TRAINING.

Considerable assistance was rendered in training the recruits by retired Sergeant Instructors of the Territorial Force who re-enlisted in the Battalion. Many of these men had previously served under Lieut.Col. Clayton and willingly came back to the Territorials, though it is doubtful if they would have offered their services in the Regular Army. They also stimulated recruiting in their own villages, and in many cases brought men with them.

The preliminary training this month consisted of physical exercises, squad drill, and route marches. Drill took place on Fairfield Common almost daily. The cold and severe weather experienced in Buxton, tried the men severely at first, but certainly hardened the physically strong.

Great keenness was displayed by the men to learn their new work and classes were held nightly by the various companies for men who were anxious to qualify for promotion.

OFFICERS.

In addition to the Senior Officers who returned with Lieut.Col. Clayton to form the Battalion, 16 Officers reported for duty with the Battalion during the month.

M Clayton
Lt. Col:
2/6 Bn. The Sherwood Foresters.

Army Form C. 2118.

WAR DIARY
or
INTELLIGENCE SUMMARY.

2/6TH BATTN. THE SHERWOOD FORESTERS.

(Erase heading not required.)

Instructions regarding War Diaries and Intelligence Summaries are contained in F.S. Regs., Part II and the Staff Manual respectively. Title pages will be prepared in manuscript.

Place	Date	Hour	Summary of Events and Information	Remarks and references to Appendices
BUXTON.	1914			
	Decr. 29th		First 120 sets of 1914 Leather Equipment issued.	
"	30th		Inspection by His Grace the Duke of Devonshire (Lord Lieutenant of the County) and H.H. the Duke of Teck.	

M. Vaughan
Lt. Col:
2/o Bn. The Sherwood Foresters.

2/6TH BN. THE SHERWOOD FORESTERS.

STATEMENT
DECEMBER 1914.

OFFICERS.

On December 2nd. Major H. Welch reported his arrival from the Depot at Chesterfield, and on the same date Capt. C.H. Heathcote reported his arrival at the Depot from Bocking, Essex, to take over duty.

On the 16th Major C.H. Heathcote reported himself for duty from the Depot, having handed over the command to Capt. T. Swann.

On the 4th and 16th respectively Lieuts. W.B.M. Jackson and H.E. Okeover were promoted to Captain, x

RIFLES.

By the end of the month 200 M.L.E. Rifles (returned by the Service Battalion) were in use for training purposes.

EQUIPMENT.

On the 29th the first 120 sets of 1914 Leather Equipment were issued.

INSPECTION.

On December 30th His Grace the Duke of Devonshire (Lord Lieutenant of the County) together with H.H. The Duke of Teck, accompanied by Col.s Broadwood, Cavendish and H. Brooke Taylor inspected the Quarters occupied by the Battalion and saw the Battalion march in.

MUSKETRY.

The work performed during this month was entirely of a preliminary nature; the men being instructed in rifle exercises, the fire positions and elementary aiming and trigger pressing. Firing on the Miniature Range did not commence until the following month.

TRAINING.

During the latter part of the month very cold weather accompanied by snow made the training of the Battalion in outdoor exercises very difficult. The time was occupied by short marches, lectures and rifle exercises etc.

MEDICAL.

The Empire Hotel, where the Unit was quartered, was a summer hotel. Severe wintry weather was experienced. Snow and rain drove in on the west side and the wind blew up through the floor boards, causing intense cold. There was an epidemic of sore throats with fever, but no accommodation could be given at the Devonshire or V.A.D. Hospitals, and many cases were sent to their respective homes to be treated locally.

Two cases of measles occurred and were promptly isolated.

There was one case of diphtheria, which required an operation, and was removed to the 3rd Northern General Hospital, Sheffield, and died there.

MEDICAL (contd).

There was an outbreak of German measles, some thirty cases occurring, the same being isolated in the Hotel, and at the Buxton Sanatorium.

The outside water-flush and sanitary arrangements were satisfactory all through the frosty weather.

Stretchers were borrowed locally, and the bandsmen were drilled with same, and also were given lectures on first aid, with detail.

Lectures were given to the Battalion on Military Hygiene, by Companies.

No cases of lice, scabies or vermin occurred.

Lt. Col:
2/6 Bn. The Sherwood Foresters.

War Diaries of
2/6th Sherwood Foresters.

January to April
and
September to December
1915.

Volume No. _____

BRITISH SALONIKA FORCE

WAR DIARY.

Att. Serbian Army.

Vol. No.	Unit	PERIOD From	To
14.	Headqtrs A.S.C. M.T. Units with S.A.	1.11.17	30.11.17
14.15.	688 M.T. Coy., A.S.C.	1.9.17	31.10.17
16.	688 do.	1.11.17	30.11.17
5.	689. do.	1.2.17	31.7.17
6.	689. do.	1.8.17	30.11.17
10.	706. do.	1.11.17	30.11.17
14.15.16.	707. do.	1.8.17	31.10.17
13.	708. do.	1.11.17	30.11.17
5.	819. do.	1.11.17	30.11.17
5.	826. do.	1.11.17	30.11.17
4.	880. do.	"	"
13.	36th General Hospital	"	"
18.	37th General Hospital	1.11.17	30.11.17
1.	881 M.T. Coy. A.S.C.	9.10.17	30.11.17

143 Bill
of Dr
1917

April
March

misc files

Army Form C. 2118.

WAR DIARY
or
INTELLIGENCE SUMMARY.

2/6TH BN. THE SHERWOOD FORESTERS.

(Erase heading not required.)

Instructions regarding War Diaries and Intelligence Summaries are contained in F.S. Regs., Part II. and the Staff Manual respectively. Title pages will be prepared in manuscript.

Place	Date	Hour	Summary of Events and Information	Remarks and references to Appendices
BUXTON.	1915.			
	Jany. 1st		The Battalion was complimented by the C.O. on its exemplary behaviour since coming to Buxton.	
"	4th		A series of lectures on Map Reading and Field Sketching for Officers commenced at Town Hall.	
"	5th		Inspection of Battalion by General Pole-Carew, Inspector General of the Territorial Forces. 1 man Discharged as Medically Unfit for further service.	
"	9th		1 man Discharged as Medically Unfit for further service. 1 man arrived from 1/6th Sherwood Foresters.	
"	12th		Organisation of Battalion changed from the 8 Company to the 4 or double Company system. 1 man discharged as Medically Unfit for further service. 5 men arrived from the 1/6th Sherwood Foresters.	
"	16th		1 man arrived from 1/6th Sherwood Foresters.	
"	20th		3 Officers proceeded to Chesterfield to raise recruits for the formation of a Third Line.	
"	21st		Brigadier General H.B.MacCall, C.B., appointed G.O.C. 1st commanding North Midland Division. Colonel Bemrose, Colonel commanding Notts. and Derby Infantry Brigade; Capt. A.N.Lee 7th Bn. The Sherwood Foresters, Brigade Major. 2 men discharged.	
"	25th		1 man attested and taken on strength of Battalion.	
"	31st		An officer proceeds to Luton to arrange billets for the Battalion.	

M.W.Taylor Lieut.Col.
2/6th Bn. The Sherwood Foresters.

2/6TH BN. THE SHERWOOD FORESTERS.

STATEMENT

JANUARY 1915.

RECRUITING.

On January 20th three Officers proceeded to Chesterfield to raise recruits for the formation of a Third Line. Offices at 103 Corporation Street, were opened as a recruiting depot. Recruiting proceeded briskly and a very good stamp of man was secured despite the fact that energetic work was being done throughout the county to obtain recruits for the new Army, thus rendering the work of recruiting for the Territorial Force more difficult than it would otherwise have been. Recruits were quickly called up and clothed as they were enrolled.

INSPECTION.

On January 19th the Battalion was inspected by Col. Bemrose, commanding the Sherwood Forester Infantry Brigade.

MUSKETRY.

Firing on the Miniature Range commenced on January 18th with No.1 Platoon; 12 men out of 40 failing to get 3 hits out of 5 at 25 yards. The range being an outdoor one, regular practice was impossible owing to weather conditions, but in spite of this, a course of 10 rounds per man throughout the Battalion was completed.

ORGANISATION.

On January 12th the Battalion was reorganised from the 8 Company to the 4 or double Company system. A and F Coys. formed the new A Coy., G and H Coys. the new B Coy., B and D Coys. the new C Coy., and C and E Coys. the new D Coys.

MEDICAL.

During this month a Sanitary Squad, Stretcher Bearers and water duty men were organised and in training. Five Lectures on Elementary Military Hygiene, and five on First Aid were given to each Company.

A number of men (50 in all) were found unfit for service and recommended for discharge.

The Medical Inspector of Recruits, Lt.Col.Jocelyn, R.A.M.C., Northern Command, inspected the Unit, and approved the discharge of several more men.

At this time the Battalion had many cases of German Measles and was suffering from an epidemic of sore throat. Foggy and wet weather had been constant for weeks, and as the second issue of boots had not yet been completed the men had suffered much from wet feet.

OFFICERS.

During the month two Officers were gazetted to the Battalion.

COURSES OF INSTRUCTION.

A series of lectures on Map Reading and Field Sketching for Officers was held during the month at the Town Hall. The Derbyshire Education Committee commenced a series of lectures at the Town Hall on various educational subjects. Special facilities were afforded to men wishing to attend.

[signature] Lt. Col:
2/6 Bn. The Sherwood Foresters.

Army Form C. 2118.

WAR DIARY
or
INTELLIGENCE SUMMARY.   2/6th Bn. The Sherwood Foresters.
(Erase heading not required.)

Instructions regarding War Diaries and Intelligence Summaries are contained in F. S. Regs., Part II. and the Staff Manual respectively. Title pages will be prepared in manuscript.

Place	Date	Hour	Summary of Events and Information	Remarks and references to Appendices
BUXTON.	1915 Feb. 3th		The Battalion moved out of Empire Hotel, Buxton, and entrained for Luton, proceeding to billets on arrival there.	W.9.R
LUTON.	Feb. 7th		2 Officers and 17 men reported their arrival from Details, 1/6th Bn. Sherwood Foresters, Ongar.	W.9.R
"	8th		The Battalion moved to Epping to undergo course of instruction in entrenching.	W.9.R
EPPING.	Feb. 9th		Entrenching commenced under instruction of C.R.E. 20 N.C.O's. and men reported their arrival from the 1/6th Bn. S.F., Braintree.	W.9.R
"	15th		One Platoon per Company composed of Imperial Service N.C.O's. and men was formed. These Platoons were fully equipped and armed with M.L.E.Rifles.	W.9.R
"	16th		10 men reported their arrival from the 1/6th Bn.S.F., Braintree. 1st Line Regimental Transport taken over from the Service Battalion.	W.9.R
"	18th		Clr.Sgt.Instr.E.Pullen proceeded to Bishops Stortford for duty at Base Depot.	W.9.R
"	19th		72 N.C.O&s. and men proceed to Braintree to join the 1/6th Bn.S.F.	W.9.R
"	22nd		7 men reported their arrival from the 1/6th Bn.S.F., Braintree.	W.9.R
"	23rd		8 men ditto. ditto.	W.9.R
"	24th		The Battalion moved to Luton.	W.9.R
LUTON.	Feb. 25th		963 Japanese Rifles and 67 boxes of 1440 rounds of Japanese ammunition received by Battalion. 1/6th Bn. Sherwood Foresters left Braintree for service overseas.	W.9.R

Lieut. Col.

Confidential

2/6th Bn. The Sherwood Foresters.

STATEMENT.

FEBRUARY 1915

OFFICERS.

2 Officers were transferred from 1/6th Bn. The Sherwood Foresters on February 7th.
2 Officers joined the Battalion on first commission.

BILLETS.

The Battalion moved out of the Empire Hotel, Buxton, on February 3rd. and occupied private billets at Luton, and Epping. During this time rations in kind were issued.

DESIGNATION.

H.M. The King graciously approved of the Notts. and Derby Infantry Brigade being designated &"The Sherwood Foresters Brigade". The Battalion designated the " 2/6th Bn. The Sherwood Foresters..

TRAINING.

On February 8th the Battalion moved to Epping for instruction in Entrenching which ended on Feb. 24th. In a letter of appreciation received by the Brigade Commander; Col. Skey C.R.E. testified to the keenness on the work and to the high standard of discipline maintained by all ranks during somewhat trying conditions whilst on entrenching work.

MUSKETRY.

The range at the Drill Hall, Epping was utilised almost daily for minature range practice and the Battalion soon showed signs of rapid improvement.

RIFLES.

On the 25th Bebruary, 963 Japanese Rifles and 67 boxes of 1440 rounds of Jap. ammunition were received by the Battalion.

TRANSPORT.

Lieut. J.H.Marsden was appointed Battalion Transport Officer on Feb.5th. On Feb. 16th the Regimental Transport of the 1/6th Bn. The Sherwood Foresters was taken over and a transport section selected.

MEDICAL.

10 cases were admitted to the local V.A.D. Hospital Epping, one ultimately classed as Enteric, was an inoculated 1/6th Battalion transfer.
Bath perades were held at the Workhouse. Field Sanitary Training was commenced and the work inspected by the A.D.M.S.

J Morton Clayton
Lieut. Col.

Army Form C. 2118.

WAR DIARY
or
INTELLIGENCE SUMMARY.

2/6th Bn. The Sherwood Foresters.

(Erase heading not required.)

Place	Date	Hour	Summary of Events and Information	Remarks and references to Appendices
LUTON.	1915 Mch. 2nd		Clr.Sgt.Instr.T.Cumming arrived from 1/6th Bn. Sherwood Foresters.	
"	4th		1 N.C.O. ditto. The G.O.C. 2/1st North Midland Division inspected the Battalion in Stockwood Park.	
"	8th		Letter "B" Company designated "Imperial Service Company".	
"	13th		10 men transferred to L/6th Bn. S.F. re-inforcement Company.	
"	19th		Signalling Section of the Battalion inspected by the Brigade Commander.	
"	20th		200 M.L.E.Rifles received.	

JMcDougloftn Lieut.Col.

Confidential

2/6th Bn, The Sherwood Foresters.

S T A T E M E N T
MARCH   1915.

INSPECTION.

On March 4th the G.O.C., 2/1st North Midland Division inspected the Battalion in Stockwood Park.

MUSKETRY.

Exceeding satisfactory range accommodation was provided in Luton, and the long stay which the Battalion made there allowed of a very comprehensive course of instruction being carried out.

A special Course of 25 rounds was fired on the Wardern Hill Range with the Japanese Rifle.

The Imperial Service platoons commenced firing Part 1, Table "A", Appendix 4, part 1, 1909 (reprint 1914) Musketry Course on Wardern Hill Range with M.L.E.Rifles.

RIFLES.

On March 20th 200 M.L.E.Rifles were received.

REINFORCEMENTS.

143 men were transferred from the 3/6th Bn. Sherwood Foresters during the month to replace drafts sent to the 1st Line.

MUSKETRY.

During the month the General Musketry Course was fired with most satisfactory results.
The men took a keen interest in their work and the Battalion topped the Brigade musketry results for this course.

MEDICAL.

Dental Treatment was arranged for. A large number of the men have received treatment and their health and fitness very much improved thereby.
Inoculation (anti-enteric) was commenced.
4 cases were sent for operation, chiefly hernia and varix, and the results were generally good.
Diphtheria was prevalent at this time and there were four cases. Two men were cerebrospinal fever contacts, but they were promptly isolated and nothing developed.

Lieut.Col.

Army Form C. 2118.

WAR DIARY
or
INTELLIGENCE SUMMARY.

(Erase heading not required.)

2/6th Bn. The Sherwood Foresters.

Place	Date	Hour	Summary of Events and Information	Remarks and references to Appendices
LUTON.	1915			
	Apl. 8th		The Battalion was inspected by Lieut.General Sir A.E.Coddrington, K.C.V.O., C.B., Commanding 3rd Army, at Stockwood Park.	
"	9yth		3 Officers proceeded to the 3/6th Bn. Sherwood Foresters for Duty.	
"	12th		43 men transferred from 3/6th Bn. S.F. 200 M.L.E.Rifles returned to Weedon.	
"	16th		A.D.V.S., 2/1st North Midland Division inspected all the horses of the Battalion.	
"v	20th		2nd Line Transport handed over to A.S.C. 100 men transferred from 3/6th Bn. S.F.	
"	27th		The Brigade Commander inspected Regimental Transport and Pack Ponies.	

G.M.Morley Taylor. Lieut.Col.

2/6TH. BN. THE SHERWOOD FORESTERS.

Confidential

S T A T E M E N T

APRIL 1915.

OFFICERS.

2 Officers joined the Battalion on first Commission.
3 Officers were transferred to 3/6th Bn. The Sherwood Foresters for duty.

INSPECTION.

The Battalion was inspected on April 8th by Lieut. General Sir A.E.Coddrington, K.C.V.O., C.B., Commanding 3rd Army, at Stockwood Park.
On April 27th the Brigade Commander inspected the Regimental Transport and Pack Ponies.

RIFLES.

200 M.L.E.Rifles were returned to Weedon on April 12th, the Battalion having a full complement of Japanese Rifles.

TRANSPORT.

The 2nd Line Transport was handed over to the A.S.C. on April 20th.

REORGANIZATION.

On March 8th the four "Imperial Service Platoons" of the Battalion were formed into one Company - Letter "B" Company - under the Command of Capt. E.B.Johnson

COURSES.

Two N.C.O's. attended a Course of Instruction in Explosives at Brentwood.
1 Officer and 1 N.C.O. attended Course of Instruction at Chelsea Barracks.

MEDICAL.

Lice (Crabs and cloths) made their appearance from billets in one area previously occupied by other troops. The Corporation Baths were available and bath parades were held.
Stretcher Bearers were Brigaded once a week for training, with good results.

Morton Clayton
Lieut. Col.

CONFIDENTIAL.

Instructions regarding War Diaries and Intelligence Summaries are contained in F.S. Regs., Part II. and the Staff Manual respectively. Title pages will be prepared in manuscript.

Army Form C. 2118.

WAR DIARY
or
INTELLIGENCE SUMMARY.

(Erase heading not required.)

2/6th Bn. The Sherwood Foresters.

Place	Date	Hour	Summary of Events and Information	Remarks and references to Appendices
WATFORD.	Septr. 1915. 1st		1 Officer (A.V.C.) attached to the Battalion for duty. Capt. The Revd. H.W.H.Ainsworth attached to the Battalion for duty.	
"	2nd		D.D.M.S. Central Force, inspected the medical and sanitary arrangements of Division. Entraining practice at Watford Goods Station North by men detailed.	
"	6th		Entraining practice with transport at L.& N.W?Goods Station, Watford. 1 Officer reported his arrival for duty.	
"	10th		1 Officer reported his arrival for duty.	
"	14th		1 Officer reported his arrival for duty.	
"	15th		Divisional Inspection by G.O.C., Division, in Gorhambury Park, St Albans.	
"	28th		Lieut.Col. L.G.Reading, A.V.C., inspected Battalion 1st Line Transport.	
"	30th		2 Officers proceeded overseas to join 1/6th Bn. Sherwood Foresters.	

A. Ashh. Major
for Lieut.Col.
2/6th Bn. The Sherwood Foresters

Confidential

2/6th Bn. The Sherwood Foresters.

S T A T E M E N T
SEPTEMBER 1915.

OFFICERS.

3 Officers joined the Battalion on First Commission.

2 Officers were attached to the Battalion for duty.

2 Officers proceeded overseas to join the 1/6th Bn. Sherwood Foresters.

COURSES OF INSTRUCTION.

1 Officer attended a Musketry Course at Bisley during the month.

The Transport Officer attended a Course of Instruction in Transport Work at Headquarters, No.3 Coy. Divisional Train, St Albans, on Septr.6th.

INSPECTIONS.

On Septr 2nd. D.D.M.S., Central Force, visited the Camp to inspect the medical and sanitary arrangements of the Brigade.

On Septr.15th, the 59th (North Midland) Division was inspected by the G.O.C. Division. The G.O.C. expressed his satisfaction with the turn out of the Division, and granted a whole holiday to the troops on the 16th.

Lieut.Col. L.G.Reading, A.V.C., inspected the Battalion 1st Line Transport on Septr.28th.

1.

TRANSPORT.

On Septr.6th the Transport Section of the Battalion practiced entraining at the L. & N.W. Goods Station, Watford.

2nd.Lt. K.H.Bond was appointed Assistant Transport Officer on Septr.11th.

MUSKETRY.

During the month the Battalion was frequently practiced on the Miniature Range.

MEDICAL.

During the month the health of the Unit continued good. A large number were vaccinated and examined as to fitness for foreign service.

Little or no difficulty was found in disposing of sullage water. Shallow earth latrines and urinals continued to be a complete success.

Watford.

H. Welch. Major
for Lieut.Col.
Cdg.2/6th Bn. The Sherwood Foresters.

Army Form C. 2118.

WAR DIARY
or
INTELLIGENCE SUMMARY.

2/6th Bn. T/aSherwood Foresters.

(Erase heading not required.)

Instructions regarding War Diaries and Intelligence Summaries are contained in F. S. Regs., Part II. and the Staff Manual respectively. Title pages will be prepared in manuscript.

Place	Date	Hour	Summary of Events and Information	Remarks and references to Appendices
WATFORD.	1915			
Octr.	1st		178th Infantry Brigade inspected by Sir Leslie Rundle, G.O.C. in C., Central Force in Gorhambury Park, St Albans.	
"	6th		Appreciation of G.O.C. in C. on Divisional Inspection published in Orders.	
"	13th		German Zeppelin raid over London. Zeppelin passed over camp. All lights extinguished, and men assembled on their alarm post at 10 p.m. as per orders.	
"	14th		Major White, Inspector of Catering, inspected Messing Books of Battalion Quartermaster, and gave Lecture on Company Messing.	
"	18th		Battalion struck Camp and went into Billets. Drill Hall used for Central Messing. Battalion Headquarters, 84, Queens Road. Quartermaster's Stores, 71, Queens Road. Battalion Alarm Post, Clarendon Road.	
"	20th		Col. Long, Inspector of Remounts, inspected Horses of the Brigade.	
"	23dr		75 Japanese Rifles withdrawn from Companies and sent to 65th Provisional Battalion, Yarmouth.	
"	26th		Armed Picquet detailed daily from date to turn out in case of an air raid.	
"	31st		Lord Bishop of Southwell conducted service and delivered an address to the Brigade.	

2/6 TH BATTN. THE SHERWOOD FORESTERS.

STATEMENT.

OCTOBER 1915.

INSPECTION.

The 178th Infantry Brigade was inspected by General Sir Leslie Rundle, G.O.C. in C., Central Force, in Gorhambury Park, St Albans on October 1st.

Considerable time has been devoted to field work during the month with satisfactory results. The number of men falling out on the heaviest days has been reduced to a minimum, proving the physical fitness of the men to endure fatigue. The experience of the field days proved that additional practice is needed in fire orders and fire control both for N.C.O's. and men.

Much attention has been paid to trenching, and during night operations useful practice has been undertaken in manning and releiving trenches. This would be rendered easier by a system of numbering the bays and traverses in the trenches in such a way that the numbers could be seen at night, and this is being undertaken.

SIGNALLING.

The strength of the Signalling Section is 46. Lamp work has been practiced once per week with the only Begbie lamp borrowed from Brigade, laying telephone lines at night and working stations. 24 men have been taken out for 2 Divisional Schemes during the month, but the equipment of the Section does not provide full work for more that 16. The Signalling Officer reports that his training would be facilitated by additional equipment. Discs necessary for classification have not been issued.

BOMB THROWING.

12 men per Company have been practiced during the month in bombing under Lt. Lawson of the 2/8th Bn.

MUSKETRY.

Miniature Rifle practice on indoor and outdoor Range has been carried out almost daily, special attention being paid to concentrated fire. The men continued to show fair progress. Rapid Fire has also been included with satisfactory results.

BILLETS.

On October 18th the Battalion struck Camp and went into private billets. The men were made very comfortable. The Drill Hall was used for central messing for the Battalion. and this system has worked smoothly.

ZEPPELIN RAID.

On October 13th a Zeppelin Raid on London was made by the Germans. One Zeppelin passed over Watford. The news of its approach was quickly circulated from Division to Brigade - thus to Battalions. Within 2 minutes all lights in Camp were extinguished. The men were removed from tents to their Alarm Post under the trees at the S.E. side of the Camp. An armed Picquet is detailed daily to turn out in case of a Raid.

OFFICERS.

Departures during October,- 4 Officers and the Battn. Chaplain proceeded overseas. ~~to join the 6th Bn. Sherwood Foresters~~.

Arrivals.- 2 Officers were gazetted to the Battalion, a Chaplain joined and 1 Captain was restored to Establishment.

RIFLES.

On Oct.23rd, 75 Japanese Rifles were withdrawn from Companies, and sent to the 65th Provisional Battn. Yarmouth.

MESSING.

Major White, Inspector of Catering, inspected the Messing Books of the Battalion Quartermaster and gave a Lecture on Company Messing. Major White expressed himself as satisfied with the messing arrangements, and the dietary of the Battalion.

BAYONET FIGHTING.

A new Bayonet Fighting Course was commenced in Cassiobury Park on October 14th. Some delay has occurred in the completion of this Course, which is not yet ready for use.

COURSES.

7 Officers proceeded on instructional courses during the month.

MEDICAL.

Camp was struck on the 18th, and the men went into billets. In camp, while the weather was chill and cold, and often very damp in the mornings, the health of the men was well maintained. Removal to Billets produced a large amount of nasal catarrh. The men were billeted in the central part of the town in a shop keeping and industrial area. They were well received and additional food and care in casual sickness was the rule, making it possible for casual cases to be treated in billets and relieve the cost on the Hospital in accordance with instructions received from Headquarters.

Vaccination was practically suspended during the month (22 men only) owing to the cold and the fact that the men crowded together at night in the tents for warmth, to the detriment of their vixicles.

Two Special Medical Boards were held during the month. 35 men were classed as Fit for Home Service, 5 for Discharged, 2 temporarily unfit, 4 fit for foreign service.

Surgical and Medical Equipment was completed by the supply of Medical Equipment, Table 26, Equipment Regulations, Part3, T.F., and one water cart, with suction pumps. 8 Stretchers were already in possession.

On moving Camp there were no untreated cases of Scabies. 15 men were being treated and in segregation. In billets the weekly inspections have been maintained, and the few men found infected were treated at once. There were no cases of Body Lice in the Unit.

Army Form C. 2118.

WAR DIARY
or
INTELLIGENCE SUMMARY.
(Erase heading not required.)

2/6TH BATTN. THE SHERWOOD FORESTERS.

Instructions regarding War Diaries and Intelligence Summaries are contained in F.S. Regs., Part II. and the Staff Manual respectively. Title pages will be prepared in manuscript.

Place	Date	Hour	Summary of Events and Information	Remarks and references to Appendices
WATFORD.	1915			
	Novr. 2nd		The Battalion moved out of private billets into hired buildings.	
"	3rd		Brigade Field Operations. 29 men certified by the Standing Medical Board as "fit for home service only" proceeded to join the 29th Provisional Battn.	
"	9th		Divisional Field Operations.	
"	10th		Major-General E.T. Dickson, Inspector of Infantry, inspected the Battalion in Musketry, bayonet fighting, bombing, trench fighting and drill (close order, extended order, rifle exercises and physical training) at Moor Park.	
"	11th		Musketry Course (Japanese) fired on Chalk Hill Range, St Albans.	
"	17th		Brigade Route March. 4 men transferred to 29th Provisional Battalion.	
"	22nd		525 Japanese Rifles handed in. 525 .303 Rifles issued to Companies. A Display of Trench warfare and bombing before the G.O.C. Division.	
"	29th		Company Training commences.	
"	25th		Divisional Concentration March.	
"	30th		Brigade Route March.	

M M Loughlin
Lt. Col:
2/6 Bn. The Sherwood Foresters

2/6TH BN. THE SHERWOOD FORESTERS.

S T A T E M E N T

NOMEMBER 1915.

OFFICERS.

Two Officers were gazetted to the Battalion, and reported for duty.

One Officer proceeded overseas, and the Veterinary Officer was struck off the strength of the Battalion on being posted to the 2/1st North Midland Brigade R.F.A.

RIFLES.

On November 22nd 525 Japanese Rifles were withdrawn from, and 525 '303 Rifles issued to Companies.

COURSES.

Three Officers attended the 3 days' Course of Instruction on Wire Entanglements held at Callowland, Watford.

One Officer proceeded to Oxford to attend the Instructional Course there, one to Kelwedon for trench fighting, and one to the Staff College.

INSPECTION.

On November 10th Major-General E.T.Dickson, Inspector of Infantry, inspected the Battalion at Moor Park, in Musketry, bayonet fighting, bombing, trench warfare and drill (close order, extended order, rifle exercises and physical training).

On November 16th the Battalion was inspected by Major-General R.N.R.Reade, C.B., G.O.C. Division, in Cassiobury Park.

BOMBING.

On November ~~18th~~ 22nd a display of trench warfare and bombing was given before Major-General R.N.R.Reade, C.B., G.O.C. Division, by the bomb throwers of the Battalion under the command of 2nd.Lt. F.Brindley, together with a party of 50 N.C.O's. and men under Lt. J.P.Maine, acting in conjunction with the other bomb throwers of the Brigade under Capt.Martyn, 2/8th Bn. The Sherwood Foresters.

BILLETS.

On November 2nd. the Battalion moved out of private billets into hired buildings, "A" and "B" Coys. occupying the Skating Rink in Clarendon Road, "C" Coy. being in the Beechen Grove Baptist School and "D" Coy. in St John's Institute.

Experience shows that the work and discipline of the Battalion are easier to keep at a high level of efficiency when the men are thus concentrated than when they are distributed in private billets.

TRANSPORT.

On November 11th the G.S.Limbered Wagons (9 in number) were taken away and G.S. Mark 10 Wagons substituted.

On November 17th the G.O.C. 59th (North Midland) Division (Major-General R.N.R.Reade, C.B.) inspected the 1st Line Transport of the Brigade (less two wagons per Battalion but including the Field Kitchens) at 10.45 a.m. in Moor Park.

MUSKETRY.

Miniature Rifle Practice has been carried out regularly during the past month in the indoor range at the Drill Hall, Clarendon Road, grouping, application and rapid practices being included in the programme, together with elementary work with Landscape Targets.

137 men attended at Chalk Hill Range on November 11th. to fire a short course (10 rounds) with the Japanese Rifle, the average being 12·6 hits per man (h.p.s.30).

MACHINE GUNS.

During the month a progressive system of training has been carried out, particular attention being directed to Signalling. The different sections have been brigaded to a great extent and have thus obtained the benefits of combined training; the progress made by the men has been very good.

SIGNAL SECTION.

There are 45 men in the Section, which is still worked on the 3 class system, but towards the end of the month, as Class C showed marked improvement, it became possible to work the two lower classes more together. There has been Buzzer practice daily for all three classes. On Novr.11th and 12th a two days' scheme was arranged; ~~the first day's scheme was arranged~~ - the first day's work being very satisfactory, Battalion Headquarters being complimented on the excellent way its signal register and files were being kept. As it rained heavily on the night 11/12th Nov. and most of the following day, the remainder of the scheme was rather spoilt.

SIGNAL SECTION (CONTD).

The latter part of the month has been occupied in working up Class A for the Classification which was held on November 30th and December 2nd. An account of this will appear in the Statement for December.

The programme of work issued on November 3rd is being adhered to as far as possible, but in two respects the work is necessarily restricted:-

(i) In lamp work, as the only Begbie Lamp in the possession of the Battalion has been withdrawn, and it has been necessary to borrow from the R.E? Signal Section whenever lamp work has to be done.

(ii) In Heliograph Work, as there is only one heliograph in the Brigade and this belongs to the R.E. Signal Section.

As only one bicycle out of 9 was fit to ride during the month, Despatch riding work has been suspended.

REGIMENTAL INSTITUTE.

The Wesleyan School, Queen&s Road, is being conducted as a Regimental Institute, and is open each evening from 6 to 9 p.m. The conveniences provided there for the comfort of N.C.O's. and men by the Committee in charge of the arrangements are highly appreciated by the Battalion.

MEDICAL.

Sickness. Under normal for November. The move into Hired Buildings has had no adverse effect. 40 men on Sick Parade weekday average. This includes men undergoing dental treatment. Each case is dealt with from day to day. Men unfit to parade in full kit are sent on duty in drill order, or in belt, as the case may require. 25 men are in Hospital.

MEDICAL (CONTD.)

    Infectious Diseases. None.

    Contagious Disease. Scabies: 33 cases (6 of them return cases). Venereal Disease: 2.

    INOCULATIONS. anti-enteric: 4; % protected 99.4%.

    Vaccinations. 32; % protected 59.8%.

    First Aid Lectures. Special Courses for Subalterns and N.C.O's. commenced November 18th.

    Eyesight, Defective. Cases have been sent to Oculist provided, but glasses ordered and said to be available under C.F.O. 1635, are not to be had.

    BILLETS.

    Messing. Clarendon Hall drains have been blocked and are still "up". The drains had to be searched for, and the disturbance has added greatly to the difficulty in keeping this large Hall clean and sweet.

    Sleeping. These are on the whole satisfactory. At the Skating Rink a better through current of air is desirable and freer facilities for this should be provided in the back wall.

    The Polytechnic (which adjoined a stable yard) was vacated in favour of the Masonic Hall.

[signature]
Lt. Col:
2/6 Bn. The Sherwood Foresters.

Army Form C. 2118.

WAR DIARY
or
INTELLIGENCE SUMMARY.   2/6TH BN. THE SHERWOOD FORESTERS.

(Erase heading not required.)

Instructions regarding War Diaries and Intelligence
Summaries are contained in F.S. Regs., Part II.
and the Staff Manual respectively. Title pages
will be prepared in manuscript.

Place	Date	Hour	Summary of Events and Information	Remarks and references to Appendices
WATFORD.	1915.			
Decr.	1st		1 man transferred to the 2/1st Northants Yeomanry.	
Decr.	6th		Armed Picquet reduced to 40 N.C.O's. and men. A Messing Committee takes over complete control of the Messing of the Battalion from this date until the end of the current pay list period.	
"	7th		Battalion Route March.	
"	10th		27 N.C.O's. and men (comprising the Band) proceed to join the 29th Provisional Battn.	
"	11th		3 men Discharged as Medically unfit for further service.	
"	14th		Brigade Route March (not completed owing to bad weather(.	
"	16th		Inspection at Grove Park by the Brigade Commander of the two Companies undergoing special training, in "General Training".	
"	17th		Inspection of the same in "Bombing" at Moor Park.	
"	18th		Do. "Bayonet Fighting" on the Final Assault Course in Cassiobury Park. The four Companies of the Battalion change over billets.	
"	20th		Inspection by the Brigade Commander of the Special Training Companies in "Night Digging".	
"	21st		Divisional Route March.	
"	29th		Battalion Route March.	

[signature] Lieut.Col.
2/6th Bn. The Sherwood Foresters.

2/6TH. BN. THE SHERWOOD FORESTERS.

STATEMENT
DECEMBER 1915.

OFFICERS.

One Officer relinquished his Commission on account of ill health.

COURSES.

Two Officers proceeded on General Instructional Courses during the month; one to Oxted and the other to St Albans.

One Sergeant and one Corporal proceeded to Bisley, the former to attend a Course at the School of Musketry and the latter the Machine Gun Course.

One Private was sent for a Course of Instruction in the repair of cycles, and one to Bermondsey for instruction in Cold Shoeing.

BILLETS.

On December 18th the four Companies of the Battalion changed over Billets, A Coy. taking over Beechen Grove and Derby Road Baptist Schools, B Coy. St John's Institute and the Congregational Hall, C & D Coys., the Skating Rink, Clarendon Road.

TRANSPORT.

During the month a full complement of G.S.Limbered Wagons (9) was reissued to the Battalion.

INSPECTIONS.

        On December 16th, 17th, 18th and 20th, Colonel E.W.S.K.Maconchy, C.B. C.I.E. D.S.O. commanding the 178th Infantry Brigade inspected the two Companies undergoing Special Training, in "General Training", "Bombing", "Bayonet Fighting" and "Night Digging".

COMPANY TRAINING.

        The results of the 3 weeks Training undergone by Letters "B" and "D" Companies have been satisfactory. Officers, N.C.O's. and men have greatly benefited by it, and it has resulted in a noticeable increase in efficiency and esprit de corps in the Companies in question.

SIGNAL SECTION.

        A Classification Test was held before the Signalling Officer at the beginning of the month. There were 19 entries, of whom 8 were passed as 1st Class and 4 2nd Class. Out of 7 failures only 2 failed hopelessly; the others only failed by a narrow margin.

        The more advanced signallers were practised continually in line testing. The Section is still very handicapped by having no lamps or dics and having to borrow from the R.E. The training has also been hindered by the very bad weather conditions, but on the whole the progress has been satisfactory.

MEDICAL.

Sickness was about normal. Quite a number of men with injury to ankle and knee through trench work. 14 men were in Hospital on December 31st.

Venereal Disease.   1 Case, Gonorrhoea.

Verminous Disease.   Scabies (17 cases, including 1 return case)
                      10 cases of Crab Lice.
                      2 cases of Clothes Lice.

These have been discovered usually at the weekly inspections, but more men are reporting voluntary where they have suspicions.

The official N.C.I. Powder and Vermigelli promised in W.O. Circular 54/Gen.No./1809 of June 1915, have never been available, although indented for repeatedly. Each soldier should have a tin of each for regular use. Suck preventative action would be of much value here in training, whilst in close billets and on the field its value would be enhanced enormously.

Medical Board was applied for but has not yet been arranged.

Special Training Companies. These have be had elementary stretcher drill and lectures on First Aid, with particular reference to control of hemorrhage.

WATFORD,
7.1.16.

Lieut.Col.
2/6th Bn. The Sherwood Foresters.

Confidential

War Diary

of

2/6th Bn. Sherwood Foresters

From 1st to 31st January 1916.

Volume

Army Form C. 2118.

WAR DIARY
or
INTELLIGENCE SUMMARY.
(Erase heading not required.)

2/6th Bn. The Sherwood Foresters.

Place	Date	Hour	Summary of Events and Information	Remarks and references to Appendices
WATFORD	1916			
	Jan. 6th		Letters "A" and "C" Companies commence Special Company Training.	
"	10th		Armr.Staff Sgt. Rabone, attached to the Battalion, transferred to 45th Provisional Bn., Margate.	
"	13th		Armr.Sgt. Kenyon, transferred from A.O.C. and attached to this Battalion.	
"	14th		Inspection of Horses by A.D.V.S., 59th North Midland Division.	
"	18th		The Major-General Commanding 59th North Midland Division inspected the Machine Gun Section of the Battalion at St Albans.	
"	21st		Divisional Operations (Administrative) at St Albans.	
"	22nd		18 Derby Recruits arrived.	
"	23rd		18 do.	
"	25th		17 do. 2 men transferred to 4th Section, 59th North Midland Division Signal Co., Royal Engineers.	
"	26th		10 Derby Recruits arrived.	
"	27th		15 do. 100 M.L.E.Rifles, III, sighted for H.V.A. were received. The Brigade Commander inspected the Special Training Companies in General Training at Cassiobury Park. Night: Letter "A" Coy. carried out test digging.	
"	28th		Inspection in Cassiobury Park of Special Training Coys. in Bayonet Fighting and Physical Training. Night: Letter "C" Coy. carried out test digging. 15 Derby Recruits arrived.	
"	29th		19 do.	
"	30th		15 do.	
"	31st		15 do.	

Morley Taylor Lieut.Col.

2/6th Bn, The Sherwood Foresters.

S T A T E M E N T.

JANUARY   1916.

COURSES OF INSTRUCTION.

During the month the following attended Courses of Instruction :-

			Commencing.
1 Officer	Grenade Work	Godstone.	Jan. 2
1 Man	School of Farriery	Woolwich	,, 3
1 Man	Cold Shoeing, Herolds Institute Bermondsey		,, 3
1 W.O.	Chelsea Barracks		,, 3
1 Officer	Musketry Course	Bisley	" 3
1 N.C.O.	Pioneer Course	Ongar	" 5
1 N.C.O.	Trench Fighting	Kelvedon	" 5
1 Man	School of Cookery	London Colney	" 5
1 Officer) 1 N.C.O.)	3rd Army Signalling School	Dunmow	" 24
1 Officer	Chelsea Barracks		" 24
1 Officer) 1 N.C.O.)	Machine Gun Course.	Bisley	" 24
1 Officer) 2 N.C.O's)	Musketry Course	Bisley	" 24

INSPECTIONS.

On Jan. 14th the A.D.V.S. 59th (N.M.) Division inspected all the horses of the Battalion.

On Jan.18th the Major General Commanding 59th (N.M.) Division inspected the Machine Gun Section of the Battalion at St. Albans.

On Jan.27th The Brigade Commander (Col.E.W.S.K. Machonchy) C.B.,? C.I.E.,D.S.O.) inspected the companies undergoing Special Training in Bayonet Fighting, Physical Training and Night Digging.

COMPANY TRAINING.

Letters "A" and "C" Companies carried out 3 weeks Special Training with satisfactory results.

MUSKETRY.

Minature Range rifle practice (grouping, application, and rapid practices) have been held during the month.

RIFLES.

On Jan. 27th. 100 M.L.E. Rifles Mark III sighted for H.V.A. were received.

LORD DERBY'S RECRUITS.

142 Recruits arrived up to Jan. 31st. the training of whom is being proceeded with in accordance with the special Training Syllabus (W.O.Letter 9/Gen. No. 5757 (M.T.2)

BILLETS.

To accommodate the Recruits, the Beechen Grove School has been taken over

BOMBERS.

During the month all available Officers and Company Sergeant Majors attended a short course of Bombing under the Brigade Bombing Officer at Moor Park.

MEDICAL.

166Sick Parades. Daily average 27. Maximum days each week were. 1 Thursday 47; 2 Wednesday 50; Tuesday 48 4. Wednesday 41: Most of the sick have reported from the companies on special training. The ailments were not serious. Catarrhs,of Phaignx and Bronchi, ankle and knee sprains,(Boils of whkch there has been quite a crop

MEDICAL.(Cont)

Dyspepsia and temporary disturbance of heart action, from the continuous strain which special training is to,same.

Falling
~~Salling~~ out on marches. The numbers are high, 10, 8 16,Nil, They are chiefly from special training companies and most of the men were obviously distressed. In four cases men fell out who had been on Sick Parade and had been ordered "Medicine and Duty"

3. Infectious and contagous Disease. There was one case of Erysiplis and billet was disinfected. Two men in Hospital were contacts of a case of Cerebro Spinal Fever and are now under observation.

There were 3 fresh cases of venereal disease and 2 recurrences, and 37 cases of scabies.

The weeklt inspection is carried out with the co-operation of O.C.Companies, the men are bathed and their bodies are clean but still the cases continue. Further measures are being taken with the bedding to reduce if possible this pest. There was one case of Crab Lice.

4. Derby Recruits. 127 arrived and have been inoculated with the new Mixed Anti Enteric vaccine.

5. Classification.of N.C.O's and men under W.O.letter 24/GenNo./4518/ A.G.1) 30.11.15. This work has occupied much time and is now nearly complete.

6. Stretcher Drill Elementary drill has been taught to the men of the training companies.

7. Field Day. 21st Jan. Thsi exercise was much appreciated and valuable lessons learnt.

MEDICAL.(Contd.)

8. Casualties in Battalion area through Aircraft

Orders are being issued for stretcher bearers and stretchers to be available at Company and Battalion Headquarters.

[signature]
Lieut. Col.

Confidential

War Diary

of

2/6th Bn. The Sherwood Foresters

from 1st to 29th February 1916.

Volume. XVI

Confidential

Army Form C. 2118.

WAR DIARY
or
INTELLIGENCE SUMMARY. 2/6th Bn. The Sherwood Foresters.

(Erase heading not required.)

Instructions regarding War Diaries and Intelligence Summaries are contained in F. S. Regs., Part II. and the Staff Manual respectively. Title pages will be prepared in manuscript.

Place	Date	Hour	Summary of Events and Information	Remarks and references to Appendices
WATFORD.	1916			
Feb.	2nd.		2/Lieut. S.C. Joyce proceeded to join the 29th Provisional Battalion Wivenhoe	Nil.
"	10th		Column inspected on the march by Lieut. Gen. Sir A. Codrington K.C., B.O., C.B.	Nil.
"	10th		Revd. E.K. Quick C.F. left the Battalion and is struck off the strength.	Nil.
"	10th		7 Officers attended before a Board for examination "Standard of Training for young Officers"	Nil.
"	26th		5 Officers attended before a Board for examination "Standard of Training for young Officers"	Nil.

M O'Mac Laghlin Lieut. Col.

Comdg. 2/6th Bn. The Sherwood Foresters.

Confidential

2/6th. BN. THE SHERWOOD FORESTERS.

STATEMENT.

FEBRUARY 1916.

COURSES OF INSTRUCTION.

The following Officers, N.C.O's. and men attended various schools of instructions during February 1916,-

		Commencing
1 Officer,	Staff College.	Feb. 8th.
1 ,,	Bisley (Machine Gun)	,, 14th.
1 Man.	Cookery Course, Bermondsey.	,, 21st.
4 N.C.O.	Ilford, (General)	,, 14th.
1 man	Woolwich, (Farriery)	,, 20th.
1 Officer.) 1 N.C.O.)	Ongar, (Pioneer Course)	,, 21st.
1 Man.	London Colney, (Cookery)	,, 23rd.

INSPECTIONS.-

On the 22nd. Feby. the G.O.C. inspected the Bombers in Moor Park during the morning, and during the afternoon of the same day an inspection of the Recruits was made in Cassiobury Park.

MUSKETRY.

Miniature Range Work has been carried out during the month.

The new Recruits have received elementry instruction in musketry, and towards the latter end of the month have been practiced on the Miniature Range.

NEW RECRUITS.-

By the 15th. of the month 208 recruits had arrived, making a total of 350. The training of these recruits is being carried out in accordance with the "Syllabus of Instructions" issued with W.O.L. 9/Gen.No. 5757/ (M.T.2.)

Confidential

BOMBERS.- A special scheme was commenced at the beginning of the month, whereby 32 men of the Companies not on special training were to receive instruction from the Battalion Bombing Officer. This system was followed until the 21st. of the month, when after an inspection by Capt. Egerton a system of training men to become instructors was adopted. This is working satisfactorily.

MEDICAL.- The inoculation against Typhoid for the whole of the 250 Recruits has been completed.

The classification of men under W.O.L. 24/Gen.NO./ 4518 was completed, and the necessary return rendered.

A Standing Medical Board was held on 11th. Feby. and ten men were recommended for discharge.

There have been fewer cases of scabies and lice at the weekly inspections, and now that a "Thrush" disinfector is being used for systematic stoving of blankets, etc. they may possibly disappear.

The Administrative Exercise held on the 9th. instant revealed many difficulties in the handling of casualties in a retiring action.

Mortimer Taylor
Lt. Col:
2/6th Bn. The Sherwood Foresters.

(2.)

www.ingramcontent.com/pod-product-compliance
Lightning Source LLC
Chambersburg PA
CBHW081453160426
43193CB00013B/2463